Let's Learn About Wudu', Ghusl, and Salah

By Asim Uysal

ERKAM
PUBLICATIONS

Erkam Publications
İkitelli Organize Sanayi Bölgesi Mahallesi
Atatürk Bulvarı Haseyad 1.Kısım No:60/3-C
Başakşehir, Istanbul, Turkey
Tel: (+90 212) 671 07 00 pbx
Fax: (+90 212) 671 07 17
E-mail: worldpublishingscom@gmail.com
Web site: http://www.islamicpublishing.net

A translation of "Abdest, Gusül ve Namaz Öğreniyorum"

The author : Asim Uysal
Translator : Joseph Shamis
Copy Editor : Suleyman Derin
Graphics : Rasim Şakiroğlu (Worldgraphics)

Contents

بسم الله الرحمن الرحيم

بسم الله الرحمن الرحيم

"Bismillahi r-Rahmani r-Rahim"

"In the name of Allah, the Compassionate, the Merciful."

Basmalah

Allah is our first word.
Our essence is full of *iman*.
When I wake every morning,
I hurry to say *bismillah*.
When I eat or drink something,
Or open my book,
I turn to my Lord,
And strength comes to my heart,
It never falls from my tongue,
Allah holds my hand.

Religious Knowledge Through Questions and Answers

Who is your Lord? Allah.

Who made you? Allah made me.

Whose servant are you? Allah' servant.

Where did we come from and where are we going? We came from Allah and we're returning to Allah.

Why were we created? To serve and worship Allah.

What must people do in their service? Worship Allah, obey the Prophet, and live Allah's religion on the earth, letting it dominate all their lives.

Since when were we Muslims? Since "*Qalu bala*" we have been Muslims, *alhamdulillah*.

What does "Qalu bala" mean? Before Allah, the Exalted, created the world, he created the souls of all people (those that have come and those that will come), gathered them into his presence and asked them:

"***Alastu bi rabbikum***" (Am I not your Lord?)

Then the souls replied

"Yes, You are our Lord," they replied, actually pledging "We will serve You and hope for Your help."

The time of this conversation is called the "*Qalu Bala*."

How many is Allah? Allah is one.

What is your religion? Islam.

Your book? The Quran "al-Karim."

***Your* qibla?** The Ka'ba.

From whose line of descent are you? From Adam's (Peace be upon him).

From whose community are you? From the community of Muhammad (pbuh).

What was his father's name? Abdullah.

What was his mother's name? Amina.

What was his wet-nurse's name? Halima.

What was his grandfather's name? Abdulmuttalib.

What was his uncle's name? Abu Talib.

Where was our prophet born? In Mecca.

When was he born? In 571 A.D.

When did the mother and father of our prophet die? Our prophet's father died two months before he was born. Our prophet's mother died when he was six years old.

How old was he when his prophethood began? His prophethood began when he was 40 and carried out his prophetic duties for 23 years.

How old was our prophet when he died? He left for the afterlife when he was 63.

Where is the grave of our prophet? In Medina.

How many children did our prophet have? Seven.

His daughters were Zaynab, Ruqiyya, Um Kulthum, and Fatimah.

His sons were Qasim, Abdullah, and Ibrahim.

Except for Fatimah, all our prophet's children died during his lifetime.

What are the prophet's wives to us? Our mothers, the mothers of all Muslims.

Who was his first wife? And who was his last? His first wife was Khadijah, and his last wife was A'ishah.

How many grandchildren did our prophet have? He had two grandsons, Hasan and Husayn, and two granddaughters, Zaynab and Umm Kulthum.

Whose children were they? They were the children of Ali and Fatimah.

32 Fards

***Iman* (Belief):** *Iman* is confirmation with the heart and confessing with the tongue. That is to say, confirmation with the heart of everything that the Prophet (pbuh) brought from Allah and saying this with the tongue.

(Amantu) The Pillars of Belief: 6

1- Belief in Allah's existence and oneness.
2- Belief in Allah's angels.
3- Belief in the books sent by Allah.
4- Belief in Allah's prophets.
5- Belief in the Last Day and the Resurrection after death.
6- Belief that the Good and the Bad come from Allah.

The Pillars of Islam: 5

1- Saying the *shahadah*.
2- Fasting in Ramadan.
3- Praying five times a day.
4- Making the Hajj, if it is *fard* (necessary) for you.
5- The paying of *zakat* (charity) by the rich on their wealth, once a year.

The Fards *(necessary obligations) for* Wudu' *(ablutions): 4*

1- Washing the face once.
2- Washing the arms up to and including the elbows.
3- Wiping a quarter of the head.
4- Washing the feet up to the ankles.

The Fards *of* Ghusl *(greater ablutions): 3*

1- Rinsing the mouth with lots of water.

2- Cleaning the nose, taking water up the nasal passages.

3- Washing the whole body, leaving no place dry.

The Fards *of* Tayammum: *2*

1- First, make the *niyyah* (intention) for *tayammum*.

2- Second, strike clean earth with your hands and wipe the face, then strike again and wipe your arms.

The Fards *of* Salah *(the Prayer): 12*

Six are for Before the Prayer, Six are for After

a- The Conditions of *Salah* (Before):

1- Purification from *hadath* (spiritual impurities): Washing away *hadath*, spiritual impurities that cannot be seen with the eye, with *wudu'*, *ghusul*, and/or *tayammum*.

2- Purification from *najasat* (physical impurities): Washing away physical impurities that may be seen with the eye from the body, the clothes, and the place of prayer.

3- *Satru l-'awrah* (Covering of the Body): Covering the parts of the body that, according to religious law, must not be seen. For men, from the navel to the knees; for women, everything should be covered except the hands, face, and feet.

4- Turning to the *Qiblah* (direction of prayer): Facing the *qiblah* during prayer.

5- Time: Praying each prayer during its prescribed time.

6- *Niyyah* (intention): Making the intention to pray the desired prayer.

b- The Conditions of *Salah* (During the Prayer):

1- The opening *takbir* ("Allahu Akbar"): Starting the prayer with "Allahu Akbar."

2- *Qiyam* (Standing): Standing while praying (if one is not disabled).

3- *Qira'ah* (Recitation): Reciting the Quran during the prayer.

4- *Ruku'* : Bowing

5- *Sujud*: Prostrating

6- *Qa'datu l-Ahirah* (Final sitting): Sitting at the end of the prayer until saying "*At-tahiyyat*."

Fard: The things that Allah commands are the *fards*, such as *salah*, fasting, and *zakah*. It is *haram* to avoid doing something that is *fard*. Someone who denies a *fard* is removed from the religion.

Sunnah: The words and deeds that, with the intention of worship, our beloved Prophet (pbuh) did often, very infrequently left undone, and recommended for us are the *sunnahs*.

Haram: The things that are forbidden, such as the drinking alcohol and the revealing of the hair by women to strange men, are *haram*. The refraining from things that are *haram* is rewarded. Someone who does things that are *haram* is a sinner. Someone that intentionally disbelieves exits from the religion.

Cleanliness for the Bathroom

- Before entering the toilet, roll up your pant cuffs so they don't get sprayed with urine, and don't pee standing up.

- Don't eat or drink anything, and don't talk.

- Enter the bathroom with your left foot; exit with the right.

Cleanliness for the bathroom: Clean yourself with your left hand and use lots of water. If there is no water, you can use something else that is appropriate.

Praying Muslims must careful attention to this type of cleanliness.

Wudu'

Wudu' is the washing of the hands, arms up to and including the elbows, and the feet, and the wiping of one quarter of the head.

***The taking of* wudu':** If possible, turn towards the *qiblah*.

Say, "I intend to take *wudu'*. *A'udhu billahi min ash-shaytani r-rajim* (I take refuge in Allah from Satan, the accursed)."

Then, wash the hands to the wrists three times in a row. While you're washing your hands, try not to leave any dry spots between your fingers. If you're wearing any rings, move them around so water can get under.

Take water into your mouth with your right hand, rinse it, then spit it out three times. Brush your teeth with a *miswak* or toothbrush, if you have one. If not, use your right thumb and *shahadah* finger.

Next, take water into your nose from your right hand three times. Use your left hand to clean it.

Wash your face, from where the hair ends to the chin, three times.

Wash your arms, first the right, then the left, from and including the elbows, three times.

Wipe one quarter of your head with the wetted palm of your right hand.

Wipe the inside of your ears with your index fingers, and the back with your thumbs.

Wipe the neck with the back of your fingers.

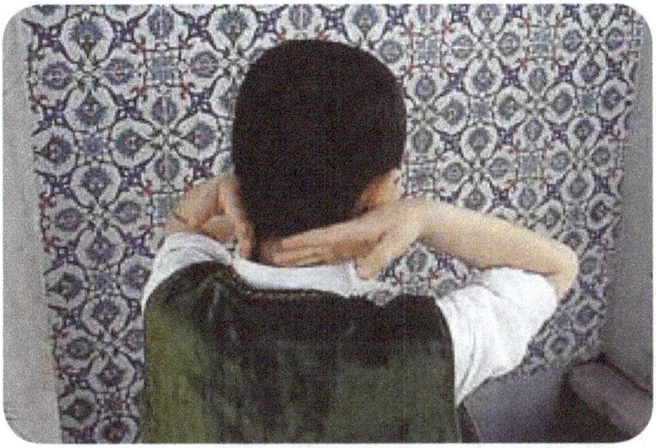

Wash the right foot, starting with smallest toe, then the left foot, up to the ankles, three times.

Thus, finishing *wudu*, it is *sunnah* to take water with the right hand and drink while standing.

After taking *wudu* it is very good to turn towards the *qibla* and say the *kalimat ash-shahada* and to read the chapter "*Inna anzalnahu*" three times.

***The* Fards *of* Wudu:**

1- Washing your face once,

2- Washing your hands, up to and including the elbows once,

3- Wiping one quarter of the head,

4- Washing your feet up to the ankles one time.

***The* Sunnahs *of* Wudu:**

1- Making the intention to take *wudu*,

2- Starting with *a'udhu* and *bismillah*,

3- Firstly, washing the hands to the wrists,

4- Cleaning the mouth with a *miswaq* and brush, or scrubbing the teeth with the thumb and index finger,

5- Washing all the parts before one dries,

6- Scrubbing the washed parts well,

7- Taking in water to the mouth and spitting it out each time,

8- When not fasting, filling the mouth with water and rinsing it around,

9- Taking water into the nose three times and taking it out by blowing the nose using the left hand, when not fasting using lots of water,

10- Taking care to go in order,

11- Washing each part three times,

12- Starting with the tips of the fingers and toes when cleaning the hands and feet,

13- Opening the fingers and toes,

14- Rubbing the beard, for someone who usually has a beard,

15- Moving around rings if there are any on the fingers,

16- Wiping the ears.

***Things that Nullify* Wudu:**

1- Filth or gas coming from the private parts.

2- Blood and pus, or blood and pus mixed with yellow liquid coming from the body.

3- Throwing up a mouthful (a spits worth does not nullify your *wudu*).

4- A spits worth or more of blood coming from the mouth.

5- Falling asleep while lying or leaning.

6- Fainting or becoming drunk.

7- Laughing loud enough while praying so that the person next to you can hear.

8- Nail polish obstructs *wudu* and *ghusl* because water cannot pass under it.

***Acts of Worship that Cannot be Done Without* Wudu:**

1- *Salah* may not be performed.

2- *The Quran* may not be touched.

3- *Tawwaf* around the Ka'bah may not be performed.

4- The *Sajdah* of *Tilawah* may not be done.

Tayammum

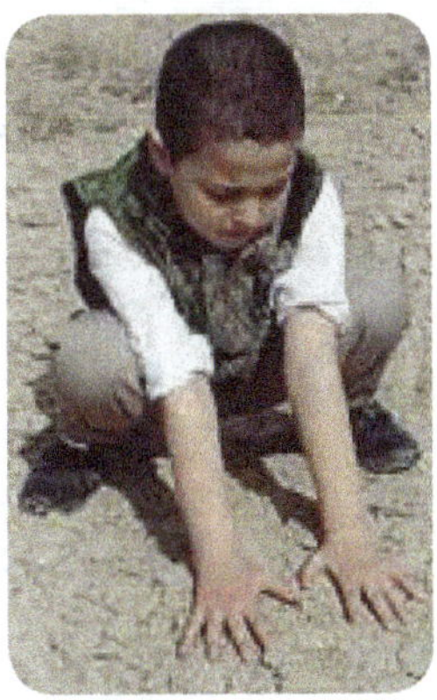

Tayammum is the wiping of your face and hands after touching clean ground.

Tayammum ***is done as follows:*** First the *a'udhu* and *basmala* are said. Then the intention is made saying, "To be clean from impurities." Then, the fingers are opened, and the palms of the hands are lightly struck against clean earth or against something made from earth. Then the hands are first placed forward, then slid back over the ground.

Note: *Tayammum* is done the same way by men and women.

The hands are first placed forward, then slid back over the ground.

The *Fards* of *Tayammum*:

1) Making the *niyyah* (intention): The intention is made by saying, "I intend to make *wudu*, to be cleansed of impurities, or to perform the *salah*."

2) Two strikes: First clean earth is struck with the hands and the face is wiped. Then they are struck again and the arms, up to and including the elbows, are wiped.

The *Sunnahs*:

1) Starting with the *basmala*.

2) Putting the hands on the ground with open fingers.

3) Rubbing the hands first to front, then sliding them back.

4) Performing it in order and not taking breaks between steps.

Taking the hands up, they may be lightly hit together to shake them off.

Every place on the face should be wiped with the palms of the hands.

Next, you should strike the earth again with the palms of your hands. First, separate the thumb and index finger of the left hand, and with the remaining three fingers of the palm wipe the inner side of the right arm up to and including the elbow.

Next, wipe the outer side of the right arm with the separated thumb and index finger of the left hand.

In the same way, this time using the right hand, wipe the right arm.

Next, with the thumb and index finger of the right hand, wipe the outer part of the right arm.

In this way, leaving no place on the face and hands unwiped, *tayammum* is done according to the *fard*s and the *sunnahs* .

Conditions Making Tayammum *Necessary:*

Any impure or menstruating person may make *tayammum* for these reasons:

1- Water is a long distance away (approximately 3,032 meters distant).

2- Because of illness.

3- Because of the cold.

4- For fear of enemies.

5- If because of a lack of water or because of a lack of

instruments, you are unable to use a sufficient amount of water for cleaning, you may do *tayammum*. If you want, you may stay in the city. It makes no difference.

If you are wearing rings, you must either take them off or move them around when you are doing *tayammum*.

Ghusl

Ghusl is the washing of the whole body.

The *fards* of *ghusl* are three:

1- *Madmada*: the taking of lots of water into the mouth up to the throat and rinsing.

2- *Istinshaq*: the cleaning of the nose by taking up water into the nasal passages.

3- Washing the body so that absolutely no dry spot remains.

For *madmada* it is also sufficient to drink a mouthful of water.

The *Sunnahs* of *Ghusl*:

1- Washing the hands and the wrists three times,

2- Washing the private parts,

3- Washing dirt off the body, if there is any,

4- Taking *wudu* like you take *wudu* for *salah*,

5- Washing the whole body three times.

6- Before *ghusl*, pouring water three times over the head, three times over the right shoulder, three times over the left shoulder, and other places,

7- Beginning with the intention in your heart and by saying "to remove the state of impurity" or "*ghusl* for the state of impurity."

8- Saying the *basmala* while washing your hands,

9- Using a normal amount of water, neither too much, nor too little,

10- While doing *ghusl*, being careful not to expose your private parts. Be especially careful to protect your private parts in public baths,

11- Scrubbing all parts well while washing,

12- Doing *ghusl* in an area where no one will see you,

13- Not talking while doing *ghusl* is *mustahab* (an action rewarded).

14- Not facing the *qiblah* while doing *ghusl*.

Performing* Ghusl *According to the* Fards, Sunnahs, *and Proper Etiquette* (adab)*:

Someone wanting to perform *ghusl* should first say the *basmala* with the intention of supplication, then make the intention to do *ghusl*. They should wash their hands to the wrists, and if there is anything stuck or dried on them they should clean it off. Then, if there is any dirt or filth around the privates or thighs, they should wash it off. Whether or not there is any filth, they should wash.

Next, taking water into the right hand, one should take water into the mouth and rinse the whole mouth, back to the throat, and between the teeth three times. Next, again from the right hand, one should suck water up the nose three times.

To rid the inside of the nose of any dirt or snot, each time one should blow out the nose into the left hand.

After that, one should take *wudu* like one takes *wudu* for *salah*. If water collects where one is standing, one shouldn't wash the feet while taking *wudu*. After *ghusl*, as one is stepping out, they may be washed. After doing *wudu*, one washes the body, pouring water three times, first on the head, then the on right shoulder, then the left. One also washes the navel and any closed earring holes. One rubs the hair, letting the water pass to the roots. If there are any wounds on the body with bandages on them, if it would be harmful to take them off, then one may let water soak in through the bandages. If that would be harmful, then they may be wiped. If wiping would be harmful, then one may leave off that also and wipe only over the bandage.

The Benefits of Ghusl:

Ghusl helps with the electrical balance of the body. It normalizes blood circulation and tension. It ensures that the pores in the skin breathe easily.

Conditions Making Ghusl *Necessary*

Ghusl is necessary for women after menstruation and childbirth and for men in a state of impurity.

While performing *ghusl*, if water reaches to the roots of a woman's hair, it is not necessary for her to undo her braids, if she has any. It is sufficient to wet the roots of the braided hair. If the braids are undone, however, it is *fard* (necessary) to wash everything.

During *ghusl*, it is necessary to move around rings and women's earrings.

After taking water into the mouth and nose, in a 45-50 square meter, still water pool, wash yourself moving the whole body three times.

If there is flowing water, *wudu* and *ghusl* may be done without moving the body.

If, on or under the nails, there is dough, nail polish, or anything that prevents water from reaching the skin, it prevents the *ghusl* from being complete.

Things that are* Haram *for Someone in a State of Greater Ritual Impurity

1- A person in a state of greater ritual impurity, menstruating women, or women who have postnatal bleeding may not enter a mosque.

2- They may not read *The Quran*.

3- They may not touch *The Quran*.

4- They may not circumambulate the *Ka'ba*.

5- They may not pray.

6- They may not fast.

Special Matters Related to Women

1- Menstruation,

2- Postnatal bleeding,

3- Withdrawal Bleeding (False Period)

Note: For more information on special matters related to women, see *İzahlı Kadın İlmihali Ansiklopedisi*, by Asim and Müşide Uysal.

The Adhan

Allahu Akbar (God is Great), four times.

Ash hadu an la illaha illa Allah (I bear witness there is no god but God), two times.

Ash hadu anna Muhammadan rasulu Allah (I bear witness that Muhammad is the Messenger of God), two times.

Hayya 'alas salah (Come fast to the prayer), two times.

Hayya 'alal falah (Come fast to salvation), two times.

Allahu Akbar (God is Great), two times.

La ilaha illa Allah (There is no god but God), one time.

During the *adhan* for *fajr* prayer, after "*hayya 'ala falah,*" "***as-salatu khayru min an-nawn***" is said twice. (meaning worship is better than sleep).

For the *iqama* (the call immediately before the prayer), "***qad qamati s-salah***" is said twice.

The *iqama* is said quickly. The *adhan* is recited loud with high volume so the Muslims in the area can hear.

This is the prayer to be said after the adhan:

Allahumma rabba hadhihi d-da'wati t-tammati, was-salatti l-qa'imati, ati sayyidana Muhammadani l-wasilata wa l-fadilata, wa d-darajata r-rafi'ata, wa b'thhu maqaman mahmudani lladhi wa'dtahu. Innaka la tukhlifu l-mi'ad.

Story: What Does Allah Want from Us?

Ahmet was in the yard helping his father mow the grass. His father said:

"Son, would you bring me a glass of water?"

As his father was drinking his water, the *adhan* began.

"Thanks Ahmet," said his father. "You did what I wanted, now Allah wants something from us."

With confusion in his eyes, Ahmet looked at his father.

"Allah wants something from us, Father?" he said.

"Yes, son."

"But I don't hear anything"

"Hey, you hear the *adhan*."

"Yes, but..."

"Son, the things Allah wants from us are made heard in different ways. For example, the *adhan* reminds Muslims about the command, "Pray!" You hear this command at every time of prayer.

The Prayer (*Salat*) is not Set in the Desert

The prayer is not set in the desert; you should pray every day
The Muslim does not set his prayer back one day.

Fajr, zuhr, 'asr, maghrib, 'isha, five times,
Stop for the prayer, let all filth drain away!

The insides of people who pray are filled with light,
The light in the faces of people who don't pray fades away.

The prayer means coming to the presence of Allah,
Talking with Allah, reaching His light.

Taking *wudu'*, clean yourself, become totally clean early;
You must become accustomed to cleanliness as a child;

A clean person is healthy, protected from illness,
Living well, laughing, as anyone who is clean.

M.Ş. Yaltkaya

The Prayer (Salah)

The Punishment for not Praying:

In a *hadith* of the Prophet (pbuh), it is related:

"A person who does not pray is between* kufr *(unbelief) and* shirk *(polytheism). That is to say, not praying is a passage leading to* kufr. *There is a way to* kufr *in not praying."

In Islam, there is absolutely no abandoning of the prayer. Even the sick do not have permission to abandon the prayer. The way that the sick pray will be explained below. In Islam, there is also no permission to abandon the prayer for those in war.

Just as there is a punishment for not praying, there is also a heavy punishment for praying without proper etiquette. Such people are called as thieves of the prayer. Among those thieves of the prayer are: those who move before the imam, those who do not fully move to bow and prostrate, etc.

In a *hadith*, the Prophet (pbuh) said:

"The worst thief among men is he who steals from his prayer."

The Times and Numbers of the Five Daily Prayers

1- ***Salatu l-fajr***: The time for this prayer continues until sunrise.

It is four *rak'ahs*, two *sunnah* and two *fard*.

2- ***Salatu z-zuhr***: The time for this prayer is when the sun comes to the very middle of the sky.

It is ten *rak'ahs*, four *sunnah*, four *fard*, and two *sunnahs* afterward.

3- *Salatu l-'asr*: The time for this prayer begins when everything's shadow is two times its height.

It is eight *rak'ahs*, four *sunnah* and four *fard*.

4- *Salatu l-maghrib*: The time for this prayer begins when the sun sets. It is five *rak'ahs*, three *fard* and two *sunnah*.

5- *Salatu l-'isha'*: The time for this prayer begins when *Salatu l-maghrib* ends, and it continues until the start of *Salatu l-fajr*. It is thirteen *rak'ahs*, four for the first *sunnah*, four *fard*, two *sunnah* afterward, and three for *Salatu l-witr* (*witr* being *wajib*).

Salatu l-witr: This is done during the time of *Salatu l-'isha'*. *Salatu l-witr* is always done after *Salatu l-'isha'*.

Fard Salah: Prayers that we pray as commanded by Allah.

Sunnah Salah: Prayers that the Prophet (pbuh) commanded and advised his followers to pray.

Wajib Salah: Between these two degrees.

Nafilah Salah: Prayers made to bring one closer to Allah.

Times in which it is *Makruh* to Pray

1- During Sunrise: If the sun rises while you are praying *Salatu l-fajr*, your prayer is nullified. It is *makruh* to pray until 45 minutes after sunrise.

2- *Zawwal*: Meaning 45 minutes before *Salatu z-zuhr*.

3- *Ghurub*: Meaning sunset. 45 minutes before the *adhan*. However it is permissible to pray the *fard* for *Salatu l-'asr* for that day while the sun is setting.

How to Pray the *Sunnah* Prayers for *Salatu l-Fajr*

1) After making *wudu'*, turning to the *qiblah*, standing straight on your feet, make your intention by saying:

"For the sake of Allah, I intend to pray the *sunnah* (or "*fard*" for the *fard*) for *Salatu l-fajr*."

The Prayer Posture and the Making of Intention:

When beginning the first *rak'ah*, the body should be relaxed, the eyes set on the place of prostration, and the feet a distance of four fingers apart.

Making the *Takbir*

2) After making your intention, say "*Allahu Akbar*" raising your hands up to the level of your ears. The palms of your hands should be facing the *qiblah* as much as possible. Then move your hands from the level of your ears and hold them below the navel.

Women make the *takbir* by raising the fingertips to the level of the chin in line with the shoulders.

Qiyam (standing) and *Qira'ah* (reciting)

3) After making the *takbir*, the right hand is placed over the left with the right hand's thumb and pinky fingers wrapped like a bracelet around the left wrist.

Women, after making the *takbir*, place their hands over the breast, with their fingers held together.

4) After placing the hands above the breast, in a very soft voice, the *subhanaka* is said:

"***Allahu Akbar. Subhanaka Allahumma wa be hamdik, wa tabaraka smuk, wa ta'ala jadduk, wa la ilaha ghayruk.***"

5) Next, the *a'udhu-basmala* is said, followed by the *Fatihah* (Opening) *Surah*:

اَعُوذُ بِاللهِ مِنَ الشَّيْطَانِ الرَّجِيمِ

"***A'udhu billahi mina sh-shaytani r-rajim.***

بِسْمِ اللهِ الرَّحْمَنِ الرَّحِيمِ {١}

الْحَمْدُ للّهِ رَبِّ الْعَالَمِينَ {٢}

الرَّحْمنِ الرَّحِيمِ {٣}

مَالِكِ يَوْمِ الدِّينِ {٤}

إِيَّاكَ نَعْبُدُ وإِيَّاكَ نَسْتَعِينُ {٥}

اهدِنَــا الصِّرَاطَ المُستَقِيمَ {٦}

صِرَاطَ الَّذِينَ أَنعَمتَ عَلَيهِمْ غَيرِ المَغضُوبِ

عَلَيهِمْ وَلاَ الضَّالِّينَ {٧}

Bismillahi r-Rahmani r-Rahim. Al-hamdu lillahi Rabbi l-'alamin. Ar-Rahmani r-Rahim. Maliki yawmi d-din. Iyyaka na'budu wa iyyaka nasta'in. Ihdina s-sirati l-mustakim. Sirat alladhina an'amta 'alayhim. Ghayri l-maghdubi 'alayhim wa la d-dallin. Amin."

6) After the *Fatihah* a short *surah* is read, for example:

إِنَّا أَعْطَيْنَاكَ الْكَوْثَرَ {١}

فَصَلِّ لِرَبِّكَ وَانْحَرْ {٢}

إِنَّ شَانِئَكَ هُوَ الأَبْتَرُ {٣}

"Inna a'taynaka l-kawthar. Fasalli li rabbika wanhar. Inna shani'aka huwa l-abtar."

Bowing (Ruku‘)

7) After the recitation of *The Quran* (The *Fatihah* and another *surah*) is finished, say "*Allahu Akbar*" and bow. In the bowing position (*ruku‘*) keep your head level with your tailbone. Keep the waist straight. The eyes should be set on the ends of the feet. The elbows should not be bent. While in *ruku‘*, you should say "*Subhana Rabbiya l-‘azim.*" This formula may be read three, five, or seven times.

As for women, they bend slightly less in the bowing position. They keep their fingers together and slightly bend their knees. They put their hands straight over their knees.

Standing: after straightening up from the bowing position, stand straight.

8) As you are straightening from the bowing position, say "*Sami'a Allahu liman hamdidah.*" After straightening, say "*Rabbana laka l-hamd.*" Stand thus for a short time, then saying "*Allahu Akbar*" move into prostration.

Prostration **(Sajdah)**

9) As you enter into *sajdah* (prostration), place, in this order, your knees, then hands, then your forehead and nose on the floor. Keep your fingers together, and keep your hands right beside your face. Keep your feet together and never take your toes off the ground. Your fingers and toes face the *qiblah.* Your knees should be far from the belly. Your elbows should not fall to the floor or connect with your belly.

Women, while in prostration, should touch their elbows to the floor and not hold their legs apart. While in *sajdah*, say "***Subhana Rabbiya l-a'la***" three times.

10) After *sajdah*, while saying "***Allahu Akbar***," straighten out into a sitting position. This sitting is called "*jalsah*." In this position, sit on your left foot while it lies pointing to the right. Hold the right foot vertical with the toes connected to the ground. Put your hands on your knees. Stay as long as it takes to say one time "*subhan Allah*."

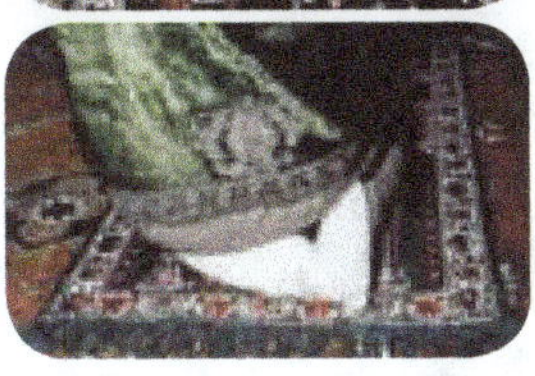

Women, while sitting, do not hold their right feet vertical, both feet lie facing the right. Afterwards, saying "***Allahu Akbar***," enter the second prostration. Again, say again "***Subhana Rabbiya l-a'la***" three times.

The Second Rak'ah

11) Next, saying "***Allahu Akbar***" (lifting first the forehead, then the hands, then the knees), without sitting, rise to your feet for the second *rak'ah*. Hold your hands together above your naval and stand still. In this way the first *rak'ah* for the *sunnah* of *Salatu l-fajr* is completed and the second one begun.

Standing and Reciting in the Second *Rak'ah*

In the second *rak'ah* "*subhanaka*" is not said. After holding the hands together, say "*Bismillahi r-Rahmani r-Rahim.*" Then, as in the first *rak'ah* the *Fatihah* is recited and another *surah* or three *ayahs* are read.

بِسْمِ اللّٰهِ الرَّحْمَنِ الرَّحِيمِ {١}

اَلْحَمْدُ لِلّٰهِ رَبِّ الْعَالَمِينَ {٢}

الرَّحْمنِ الرَّحِيمِ {٣}

مَالِكِ يَوْمِ الدِّينِ {٤}

إِيَّاكَ نَعْبُدُ وإِيَّاكَ نَسْتَعِينُ {٥}

اهدنَـا الصِّرَاطَ الْمُستَقِيمَ {٦}

صِرَاطَ الَّذِينَ أَنعَمتَ عَلَيهِمْ غَيرِ المَغضُوبِ

عَلَيهِمْ وَلاَ الضَّالِّينَ {٧}

Bismillahi r-Rahmani r-Rahimm. Al-Hamdu lillahi rabbi l-'alamin. Ar-Rahmani r-Rahim. Maliki yawmi d-din. Iyyaka na'budu wa iyyaka nasta'in. Ihdina s-sirata l-mustakim. Sirata lladhina an'amta 'alayhim. Ghayri l-maghdubi 'alayhim wa la d-dallin. Amin.

قُلْ هُوَ اللَّهُ أَحَدٌ {١}
اللَّهُ الصَّمَدُ {٢}
لَمْ يَلِدْ وَلَمْ يُولَدْ {٣}
وَلَمْ يَكُن لَّهُ كُفُواً أَحَدٌ {٤}

Surat al-ikhlas: ***Qul huwa Allahu ahad. Allahu s-Samad. Lam yalid wa lam yulad. Wa lam yakullahu kufuwan ahad.***

Bowing (Ruku')

12) Next, saying "***Allahu Akbar*** move to the *ruku'* (bowing) position. In *ruku'* say, "***Subhana Rabbiya l-'azim***" three times. Then saying "***Sami'a Allahu liman hamidah***"

stand back up. After saying "***Rabbana laka l-Hamd,***" say "***Allahu Akbar***" and prostrate.

As for women, they bend slightly less in the bowing position. They keep their fingers together and slightly bend their knees. They put their hands straight over their knees.

Prostrating (Sajdah)

13) Next, after saying in the *sajdah* (prostration) position "***Subhana Rabbiya l-a'la***" three times, say "***Allahu Akbar***" and straighten up to the sitting position. Then repeat "***Allahu Akbar***" and move to the second *sajdah*. Say again three times "***Subhana Rabbiya l-a'la.***" Then say "***Allahu Akbar***" and move back to the sitting position for the "***Tahhiyyat.***"

Women, while in prostration, should touch their elbows to the floor and not hold their legs apart. While in *sajdah*, say "***Subhana Rabbiya l-a'la***" three times.

The Tahiyyat

After *sajdah*, return to the sitting position while saying "***Allahu Akbar***." This sitting is called "*qa'idat al-akhirah*" (the last sitting). For men, the toes point toward the *qiblah* and the right foot is up. Lay your left foot sideways and sit on it. The hands are left to lie freely on the knees. Set the eyes on your lap and read the "***At-tahiyyat***" *du'ah*.

The way of sitting is different for women. Women put both their feet out facing to the right and sit on their left femur. Their hands, with fingers together are rested on their knees.

At-tahiyyatu lillahi wa s-salawatu wa t-tayyibatu, as-salmu 'alayk, ayyuha n-nabiyyu wa rahmat Allahi wa barakatuh, as-salamu 'alayna wa 'ala 'ibadillahi s-salihin. Ashhadu an la ilaha illa Allah wa ashhadu anna Muhammadan 'abduhu wa rasuluh.

In the last sitting, after the *at-tahiyyat du'ah*, the "*Salli, barik wa rabbana*" *du'ah* is read.

- ***Allahumma salli 'ala sayyidina Muhammadin wa 'ala ali sayyidina Muhammadin kama sallayta 'ala Ibrahima wa 'ala ali Ibrahima, innaka hamidun majid.***

- ***Allahumma barik 'ala Muhammadin va 'ala ali Muhammadin kama barakta 'ala Ibrahima wa 'ala ali Ibrahima, innaka hamidun majid.***

- ***Rabbana atina fi d-dunya hasanatan wa fi l-akhirati hasanatan wa qina 'adhaba n-nar.***

Rabbana ghfirli wa li walidayya wa li l-mu'minina yawma yaqumu l-hisab.

15) When this *du'ah* is finished, turn your head to the right, with your eyes looking over your right shoulder, and say, "***As-salamu 'alaykum wa rahmatullah.***" Then turn your head to the left, with your eyes looking over your left shoulder, and say, "***As-salamu 'alaykum wa rahmatullah.***"

In this way the two-*rak'ah* *sunnah* or *fard* prayer for *salat al-fajr* is finished. After the *fard* prayer, the recommendation of the Prophet (pbuh) is to say three times:

"***Astaghfirullaha l-'azim.***" ("O Allah! I beseech you for the forgiveness of my sins.")

The Du'a *and* Tesbih *after the Prayer:*

Allahumma anta s-salamu wa minka s-salam. Tabarakta ya dha l-jalali wa l-ikram.

'Ala rasulina salawat.

(Allahumma salli 'ala sayyidina Muhammadin wa 'ala ali sayyidina Muhammad.) said to oneself, silently.

Subhan Allahi wa l-hamdu lillahi wa la ilaha illa Allahu wa Allahu Akbar. Wa la hawla wa la quwwata illa billahi l-'aliyyi l-'azim.

After this, the *a'udhu-basmalah* is said together with *Ayat al-Kursi* (The Throne Verse). Then these *tasbih duahs* are said:

Tesbihs:	Translations:
Subhanallah: 33 times	Glory be to God.
Alhamdulillah: 33 times	Praise be to God.
Allahu Akbar: 33 times	God is the Greatest.

Allahu Akbar. La ilaha illahu, wahdahu, la sharikah lah. Lahu l-mulk wa lahu l-hamdu wa huwa 'ala kulli shay'in qadir.

A General Du'ah *to be read after the prayer:*

A'udhu billahi mina sh-shaytani r-rajim. Bismillahi r-rahmani r-rahim.

Praise be to the Lord of the worlds, and peace and blessings be upon our Master Muhammad, and on his family and companions. We praise Him and seek his help, and we turn to him in repentance. It is certain that he accepts much repentance and forgives the believers much in the hereafter.

O my Lord! Accept our prayers and worship, together with our faults.

O my Lord! Forgive us our sins, have mercy on us, take us into paradise and protect us from the fire of hell.

O my Lord! Make all our works pleasing to You.

O my Lord! Help Islam and Muslims.

O my Lord! Protect us from unbelief, polytheism, poverty, and the trial of the grave.

O my Lord! I ask of you long life, beneficial knowledge and peace in this world and the next.

(At this time, you may say whatever it is you desire from Allah)

O my Lord! On the Day of Judgement, protect me, my mother and father and all believers with your mercy, O Allah, the Merciful, the Compassionate.

Amen! Amen! O my Lord! Accept my prayers.

Say, "***Subhana Rabbika, Rabbi l-'izzati 'amma yasifun wa salamun 'ala l-mursalin, wa l-hamdu lillahi Rabbi l-'alamin. Al-Fatihah***" and afterwards say the *a'udhu-basmalah* with *The Fatihah.*

How to Pray Salat az-Zuhr

Salat az-Zuhr is ten *rak'ahs*, four *rak'ahs* for the first *sunnah*, four *rak'ahs* *fard*, and two *rak'ahs* for the last *sunnah*.

The First *Sunnah* for *Salat az-Zuhr*: The first *sunnah* is four *rak'ahs*. Say, "For the sake of Allah, I intend to pray the first *sunnah* prayer for *salat az-zuhr*." After praying two *rak'ahs*, just as is done for the *sunnah* prayer for *salat al-fajr*, sit and say the *at-tahiyyat*.

After that, without saying anything else, say "*Allahu Akbar*" and stand again for the third *rak'ah*. The third *rak'ah* starts with only the *basmalah*, and, as you sit after reciting *The Fatihah* and a *surah* in the first two *rak'ahs*, do likewise in the third and fourth *rak'ahs*. Say the *tahiyyat*, "*Allahumma salli*," "*Allahumma barik*," and "*Rabbana atina*" *du'ahs* till the end, then give *salams*.

The *Fard* for *Salat az-Zuhr*: The *fard* for this prayer is four *rak'ahs*. Say, "For the sake of Allah, I intend to pray the *fard* prayer for *salat az-zuhr*." It is like the first *sunnah* prayer for *salat az-zuhr*. In the third and fourth *rak'ahs*, only *The Fatihah* is read. Another *surah* or *ayah* is not read.

First *Rak'ah*:	**Second *Rak'ah*:**	**First Sitting:**
Iqamah (for men)	*Basmalah*	*at-Tahiyyat*
Niyyah	*Fatihah*	
Takbir	A *surah*	
Subhanaka	*Ruku'*	
A'udhu-Basmala	*Sajdah*	

Fatihah		
A *surah*		
Ruku‘		
Sajdah		

Third *Rak‘ah*:	**Fourth *Rak‘ah*:**	**Final Sitting:**
Basmala	*Basmala*	*at-Tahiyyat*
Only *Fatihah*	*Fatihah*	*Allahumma salli*
Ruku‘	*Ruku‘*	*Allahumma barik*
Sajdah	*Sajdah*	*Rabbana*
		Salam

Note: The *fard* prayers for *salat az-Zuhr, salat al-‘asr, and salat al-‘isha* are all prayed in the same way.

The Final *Sunnah* prayer for *Salat az-Zuhr*: The final *sunnah* prayer is two *rak‘ahs*. Say, "For the sake of Allah, I intend to pray the last *sunnah* prayer for *salat az-zuhr*."

Note: They way to pray this prayer is the same as for the *sunnah* prayer for *salat al-fajr*. Refer to that for the details. It is prayed the same as the *sunnah* prayer for *salat al-maghrib* and the final *sunnah* prayer for *salat al-'isha.*

How to Pray *Salat al-'Asr*

Salat al-'asr is eight *rak'ahs*, four *rak'ahs sunnah* and four *rak'ahs fard.*

The *Sunnah* Prayer for *Salat al-Asr*: The *sunnah* prayer is four *rak'ahs*. Make your intention by saying, "For the sake of Allah, I intend to pray the *sunnah* prayer for *salat al-'asr.*" This is like the *sunnah* prayer for *salat az-Zuhr*, except in the second *rak'ah*, after saying the *tahiyyat*, you continue with *Allahumma sallli/barik*. After that, saying "*Allahu Akbar*," raise for the third *rak'ah* and, as if you're starting the prayer again, say the *subhanaka* and *a'udhu-basmala*, then the *Fatihah* and a *surah*.

The *Fard* Prayer for *Salat al-'Asr*: This prayer is four *rak'ahs*. Make your intention by saying, "For the sake of Allah, I intend to pray the *fard* prayer for *salat al-'asr.*" It is prayed like the *fard* for *salat az-Zuhr*.

How to Pray *Salat al-Maghrib*

***Salat al-Maghrib* is five *rak'ahs*:** three *fard*, and two *sunnah.*

The *Fard* for *Salat al-Maghrib*: The *fard* for this prayer is three *rak'ahs*. Say, "For the sake of Allah, I intend to pray the *fard* prayer for *salat al-maghrib.*" After praying the first two *rak'ahs* as you would for the *fard* for *salat al-fajr* and sitting and saying the *tahiyyat*, stand again for the third *rak'ah*. In the third *rak'ah*, say only the *Fatihah*. When sitting, say the *tahiyyat* and the *salli, barik* and *rabbana duas*, and say *salam*.

The *Sunnah* for *Salat al-Maghrib*: The *sunnah* for this prayer is two *rak'ahs*. Say, "For the sake of Allah, I intend to pray the *sunnah* prayer for *salat al-maghrib*." It is the same as the *sunnah* prayer for *salat al-fajr*. Refer to that for details.

How to Pray *Salat al-'Isha*

Salat al-'Isha: This prayer is ten *rak'ahs*, four *rak'ahs* first *sunnah*, four *rak'ahs fard*, and two *rak'ahs* second *sunnah*.

The First *Sunnah* for *Salat al-'Isha*: The first *sunnah* is four *rak'ahs*. Make your intention by saying, "For the sake of Allah, I intend to pray the first *sunnah* prayer for *salat al-'isha*." Pray it like the *sunnah* for *salat al-'asr*.

The *Fard* for *Salat al-'Isha*: The *fard* is four *rak'ahs*. Make your intention by saying, "For the sake of Allah, I intend to pray the *fard* prayer for *salat al-'isha*." Pray it like the *fard* for *salat az-zuhr* or *salat al-'asr*.

The Final *Sunnah* for *Salat al-'Isha*: The final *sunnah* is two *rak'ahs*. Make your intention by saying, "For the sake of Allah, I intend to pray the final *sunnah* prayer for *salat al-'isha*."

Note: It is prayed the same way as the *sunnah* prayer for *salat al-fajr*. Look there for details. The *sunnah* prayers for *salat al-maghrib* and the last *sunnah* prayers for *salat al-'asr* are the prayed the same way.

Salat al-Witr

***Salat al-Witr* is three *rak'ahs*.** The first two *rak'ahs* are prayed the same as the first two *rak'ahs* for the *sunnah* of *salat al-fajr*, except that after the second *rak'ah*, when you are sitting, you say only the *tahiyyat* before rising for the third *rak'ah*.

In the third *rak'ah*, after saying the *Fatihah* and reading another *surah*, raise your hands to the level of your ears, say the *takbir*, then hold your hands again below the navel. At this time you read the *qunut du'ah*. It is time for the *surahs* after you read the *qunut du'ah*. After finishing this *du'ah* and going into the bowing and prostrating positions, finish the prayer in the normal way.

If you do not know the *qunut du'ah*, you should say "***Allahumma ghfir li***" before bowing.

How to Pray the Three *Rak'ahs* of *Salat al-Witr*

First *Rak'ah*:	**Second *Rak'ah*:**	**First Sitting:**
Niyyah	*Basmalah*	*at-Tahiyyat*
Takbir	*Fatihah*	
Subhanaka	A *surah*	
A'udhu-Basmalah	*Ruku'*	
Fatihah	*Sajdah*	
A *Surah*		
Ruku'		
Sajdah		

Third *Rak'ah*:	***Takbir* Interlude**	**Final Sitting:**
Basmalah	*Takbir* interlude and *Qunut dua*	*at-Tahiyat*
Fatihah	*Qunut Duas*	*Allahumma salli*
A *Surah*	*Ruku'*	*Allahumma barik*
	Sajdah	*Rabbana*
		Salam

The *Fards* of the Prayer

These are listed in the beginning of the book under the title "32 *fards*."

Things that Nullify the Prayer

1- Thinking about something related to this world and uttering a sound, or saying "Ouch!" or "Ah!" because of some pain, soreness, or tiredness.

2- Trying to cough when you do not need to.

3- Blowing or puffing on something.

4- Reading an *ayah* with the intention of responding to someone.

5- The ending of the time period allowable for wearing leather slippers, (Mash).

6- Saying "Get!", "Go away!," or something similar to a cat or dog trying to get it to go away.

7- Swallowing snow, rain, or sleet that falls into your mouth during the prayer.

8- Reading an *ayah* incorrectly, changing the meaning.

9- For men, standing beside women.

10- Scratching the same place three times while praying in the bowing position.

11- If an area that should be covered is uncovered for the time it takes to perform one *ruku'* (bowing) or if something dirty falls on your clothes that stops the prayer.

12- Suddenly lifting both of your feet up from the ground while in *sajdah* (prostration).

13- Seeing menstruation while praying.

14- If the sun rises while you are praying *salat al-fajr*.

15- Talking during the prayer, because of forgetfulness, by mistake or knowingly.

16- Eating or drinking something while you're praying.

17- Laughing loud enough so you can hear it yourself. (If you laugh loud enough so those around you can hear it, it also nullifies your *wudu'*.)

18- Turning your breast away from the *qiblah*.

19- Trying to do some kind of work while you are praying.

Sajdah (Prostration) of Forgetfulness

The *sajdah al-sahw* means "the prostration of forgetfulness." It completes or eliminates anything missing or extra that we forget or do during the prayer unknowingly or because of forgetfulness.

Sajah al-sahw is used in three cases:

1- The delaying of a *fard*.

2- The leaving off of a *wajib*.

3- The delaying of a *wajib*.

How the prostration of forgetfulness is done: In the final sitting of the *salah* you are praying (in the sitting where you say *salams*), read the *tahiyyat*. Then directly after saying *salam* towards both directions, say "*Allahu Akbar*," go into *sajdah* (prostration) two times, and sit again. Say the *tahiyyat*, *allahummas*, and the *rabbana du'as* again, and say the *salams* in both directions, and your prayer is made complete.

A *Surah* to be Read After *Salat al-Fajr*

هُوَ اللَّهُ الَّذِي لَا إِلَهَ إِلَّا
هُوَ عَالِمُ الْغَيْبِ وَالشَّهَادَةِ هُوَ الرَّحْمَنُ الرَّحِيمُ {٢٢}
هُوَ اللَّهُ الَّذِي لَا إِلَهَ إِلَّا هُوَ الْمَلِكُ الْقُدُّوسُ السَّلَامُ الْمُؤْمِنُ
الْمُهَيْمِنُ الْعَزِيزُ الْجَبَّارُ الْمُتَكَبِّرُ سُبْحَانَ اللَّهِ عَمَّا يُشْرِكُونَ {٢٣}
هُوَ اللَّهُ الْخَالِقُ الْبَارِئُ الْمُصَوِّرُ لَهُ الْأَسْمَاءُ الْحُسْنَى
يُسَبِّحُ لَهُ مَا فِي السَّمَاوَاتِ وَالْأَرْضِ وَهُوَ
الْعَزِيزُ الْحَكِيمُ {٢٤}

Bismillahi r-Rahmani r-Rahim.

Huwa Allahu lladhi la ilaha illa huw. 'Alimu l-ghaybi wa sh-shahadati huwa r-rahmanu r-rahim. Huwa Allahu lladhi la ilaha illa huw. Al-maliku l-quddusu s-salamu l-mu'minu l-muhayminu l-'azizu l-jabbaru l-mutakabbir. Subhana Allahi 'amma yushrikun. Huwa Allahu l-khaliqu l-bari'u l-musawwiru lahu l-asma'u l-husna. Yusabbihu lahu ma fi s-samawati wa l-ard. Wa huwa l-'azizu l-hakim.

A *Surah* to be Read After *Salat al-'Isha*

آمَنَ الرَّسُولُ بِمَا أُنزِلَ إِلَيْهِ
مِن رَّبِّهِ وَالْمُؤْمِنُونَ كُلٌّ آمَنَ بِاللّهِ وَمَلآئِكَتِهِ
وَكُتُبِهِ وَرُسُلِهِ لاَ نُفَرِّقُ بَيْنَ أَحَدٍ مِّن رُّسُلِهِ وَقَالُواْ سَمِعْنَا
وَأَطَعْنَا غُفْرَانَكَ رَبَّنَا وَإِلَيْكَ الْمَصِيرُ {٢٨٥} لاَ يُكَلِّفُ اللّهُ نَفْساً
إِلاَّ وُسْعَهَا لَهَا مَا كَسَبَتْ وَعَلَيْهَا مَا اكْتَسَبَتْ رَبَّنَا لاَ تُؤَاخِذْنَا إِن
نَّسِينَا أَوْ أَخْطَأْنَا رَبَّنَا وَلاَ تَحْمِلْ عَلَيْنَا إِصْراً كَمَا حَمَلْتَهُ عَلَى
الَّذِينَ مِن قَبْلِنَا رَبَّنَا وَلاَ تُحَمِّلْنَا مَا لاَ طَاقَةَ لَنَا بِهِ وَاعْفُ
عَنَّا وَاغْفِرْ لَنَا وَارْحَمْنَا أَنتَ مَوْلاَنَا فَانصُرْنَا عَلَى
الْقَوْمِ الْكَافِرِينَ {٢٨٦}

Bismillahi r-Rahmani r-Rahim.

Amana r-rasulu bima unzila ilayhi min rabbihi. Wa l-mu'minuna kullun amana billahi wa mala'ikatihi wa kutubihi wa rusulihi, la nufarriqu bayna ahadim min rusulihi. Wa qalu sami'na wa ata'na ghufranaka rabbana wa ilayka l-masir. La yukallifullahu nafsan illa wus'aha, laha ma kasabat wa 'alayha ma ktasabat. Rabbana la tu'akhidhna in nasina aw akhta'na. Rabbana wa la tahmil 'alayna isran kama hamaltahu 'ala lladhina min qablina. Rabbana wa la tuhammilna ma la taqata lana bih. Wa'fu 'anna wa ghfir lana wa rhamna. Anta mawlana fansurna 'ala l-qawmi l-kafirin.

Ruling About Praying in Congregation (*Jam'at*) : The reward for the prayer of someone who prays in congregation is twenty-five (or according to one narration twenty-seven) times greater than that of someone who prays alone. For this reason, whenever two or more people come together, they should pray in congregation.

Different Prayers Besides the Five Daily Prayers

***Salat al-Jum'ah*:** The time for this prayer is the same as that for *salat az-zuhr*. It is two *rak'ahs* prayed together in congregation in place of *salat az-zuhr*. It is ten *rak'ahs* in total.

There are a total of eight *rak'ahs sunnah*: four before the *fard* and four after. After the time for the prayer begins, first pray four *rak'ahs sunnah*. After the *khutbah*, pray two *rak'ahs* for *salat al-jum'ah* in congregation. After these two *rak'ahs fard*, pray four more *rak'ahs sunnah*.

After this, it is best if you pray two *rak'ahs* intending to pray "*waqt sunnati*."

Conditions for *Salat al-Jum'ah* to be *Fard*:

1- It is *fard* for men, it is not *fard* for women. However, if a woman is present at *salat al-jum'ah* and she prays *salat al-jum'ah* with the imam, it counts for *salat az-zuhr*.
2- The way to *salat al-jum'ah* must be open and free.
3- You must not be a traveler.
4- You must not be sick, but be healthy.
5- You must not be blind.
6- You must not have a good excuse for not going.

Conditions for *Salat al-Jum'ah* to be *Sahih* (valid)

Just as there are some necessary conditions for *salat al-jum'ah* to be *fard*, there are also some conditions for it to be *sahih*.

1) *Salat al-jum'ah* must be prayed during the time for *salat az-zuhr*.
2) The *khutbah* must be read before the prayer.
3) The place where *jum'ah* is prayed must be open to everybody.

4) Besides the imam, there must be a minimum of three other men. (According to Imam Abu Yusuf, it is *sahih* if two men are there.)

5) A person authorized to lead the prayer must be found.

6) The place where *jum'ah* is prayed must be a city or connected to the city government.

Salat al-'Id

For people for whom *salat al-jum'ah* is *fard*, it is *wajib* to pray the two *salat al-'id*s in the year.

Salat al-'id is two *rak'ahs*. This is also prayed in congregation. When the sun rises two spear-lengths above the horizon, the time for *salat al-'id* begins. When the time begins, the congregation makes their intention by saying sincerely, "I intend to pray *salat al-'id*, which is *wajib*, following the imam."

Salat al-Musafir (Traveler's Prayer)

A person is consider a *musafir* (traveler) once he leaves his village, town, or camp, intending to make a journey somewhere, traveling at a medium pace for at least three days (meaning an 18 hour journey or 90 km) .

If the traveler intends to stay at his place of arrival for 15 days or more, he is no longer considered a traveler. If he plans to stay for less than 15 days, then he is still considered a traveler. If he says, "I'm going to leave today" or "I'm going to leave tomorrow," then even if he stays for ten years, he will still be considered a traveler.

Travelers pray two *rak'ahs* in place of *fard* prayers that have four *rak'ahs*. Three and two *rak'ah* prayers are prayed in full. When safe stopping places are found and there is enough time, *sunnahs* are prayed as usual.

The Door to Islam:

"*al-kalimat at-tawhid* and *al-kalimat ash-shahadah*"

How does one become a Muslim?

One becomes a Muslim by saying *al-kalimat at-tawhid* and *al-kalimat ash-shahadah* and sincerely believing it.

What is the essence of the religion of Islam?

Al-kalimat at-tawhid.

Al-Kalimat at-Tawhid:

"*La ilaha, illallah, Muhammadun rasulullah*"

Translation: "There is no god besides God (Allah), and Muhammad (pbuh) is his Messenger."

***La ilaha* (There is no god(s)):** I swear that I will not accept those gods that people made themselves and that I will purify my heart from them for Allah. I am preparing my heart, purified from other gods, only for Allah and his religion. This must be done because an impure heart cannot hold pure belief in Allah, just as a sound building cannot be built upon a rotten foundation.

Illa Allah: After rejecting false gods, I accept only Allah as my Lord.

***Muhammadun Rasulullah*:** This means "This worship of my Lord is not done according to *bid'ah* (later innovations in the religion). It is done according to the way that *The Quran* shows, that the Messenger taught, and in the way that the Messenger has shown us."

Kalimat ash-Shahadah:

"*Ashhadu an la ilaha illa Allah wa ashhadu anna Muhammadan 'abduhu wa rasuluhu.*"

Translation: I bear witness that there is no god but Allah and that Muhammad (pbuh) is his servant and Messenger.

***Ashhadu an la ilaha illa Allah*:** This means "I think, understand, accept in my heart, and say with my tongue that there is no god (i.e. power, possessor of absolute power, legislator and subduer of the universe and all the people in it) but Allah. If someone says, 'I exist in spite of Allah,' this means: I reject Allah and do not know Him.'"

Faith in Allah

Story: **Allah Sees Us:**

Salih asked his uncle:

- Why can't we see Allah?

His uncle replied:

- We don't see Allah because our eyes were not made to see Him."

- But, how is that, my dear uncle?

- Can you take a picture of anything with your camera?

- Yes. I can.

- Can you also take a picture of your liver, lungs and stomach?

- No, an X-ray machine can take pictures of that.

- What I mean is each of them, when they're taking pictures, don't take the picture seen by the X-ray machine because each is taken differently. Allah didn't make us so we could see him.

- Does He see us?

- Yes, in a dark night, in a dark room, even if we're wearing black clothes, He sees us.

Allah's Attributes *(Sifat)*

A- ***as-Sifat adh-dhati***, B- ***as-Sifat ath-thatubi***

A- ***as-Sifat adh-dhati***: These are six in number.

1- *Wujud*: This means existence. Allah exists everywhere at all times.

2- *Qidam:* Allah's existence has no beginning. Allah has no beginning, he is pre-eternal.

3- *Baka'*: There will never be an end to His existence. Allah has no end, he is eternal. He is immortal.

4- *Wahdaniyyah*: This means "to be one." This means that it is impossible to find His attributes and actions in a different being. Allah has no partner or one like Him.

5- *Mukhalafatun li l-hawadith*: This means that nothing that is later created is like Him. Allah is not like anything that is made afterward.

6- *Qiyam bi Nafsihi*: (*Qiyam bi dhâtihi*): Allah's existence is from Himself. He has no need of any other existence. Everything is in need of him.

B- *As-Sifat ath-Thabuti*: These are eight in number.

1- *Hayât*: This means "to be living." Allah is the possessor of life and living.

2- *'Ilm*: This means "to know." Allah knows everything.

3- *Sami'*: This means "to hear." Allah hears everything.

4- *Basar*: This means "to see." Allah sees everything.

5- *Iradah*: This means "to wish" or "to want." Allah is free to wish and want whatever He likes.

6- *Qudrah*: Allah is the possessor of power (*qudrah*). Allah's power is sufficient for everything.

7- *Kalâm*: Allah has the attribute of speech. Allah talks to whom He wants and says what He wants.

8- *Takwin*: This means "to make" or "to create." Allah made everything on the earth and in the sky.

Questions Related to Allah's Attributes

Who is your creator?	**Allah**
Who sees everything?	....
Who hears everything?	....
Who knows everything?	....
Who provides for everything?	....
Who has the power to do everything?	....
Who is everywhere?	....
Whose existence has no beginning?	....
Whose existence has no end?	....
Who has no like or equal?	....
Who has no partners?	....
Who needs no one else?	....
Who is immortal?	....
Who is omnipotent (all-powerful)?	....
Who was not born and does not beget?	....
Who protects us?	....
Who forgives us?	....
Who gives us life?	....
Who is your Lord?	....
Who is the Greatest?	....
Who is the Most Beautiful?	....
Whom do we love most?	....
Who helps us when times are hard?	....
Whom do we ask to protect us when we fear?	....
Who nurtures us and raises us?	....
Who protects us from dangers?	....

Allah is the Creator of Everything.

Who created the world?	Allah
Who created the stars?	....
Who created the moon?	....
Who created the sun?	....
Who created the earth, the sky, and the air?	....
Who holds the stars in the sky set in order?	....
Who makes it rain?	....
Who created people from nothing?	....
Who created me?	....
Who created my mom and dad?	....
Who created the animals?	....
Who created the plants?	....
Who created the mountains?	....
Who created fruits and vegetables?	....
Who provides us with sustenance and blessings?	....
Who makes living plants from dead soil?	....
Who brings out various flowers and differing scents from the same origin?	....
Who kills the living?	....
Who created everything?	....
Who is the owner of the universe?	....

Our Duties to Allah:

1- To believe only in Allah, and not attach partners to Him,

2- To love Allah with the heart more than everyone else,

3- To turn only to Allah for forgiveness of sins,

4- To rely only on Allah, to ask only Him for help,

5- To continually worship Him alone.

6- To be thankful to Him for the bounties He bestows,

7- To love those He loves and hate those He hates.

8- To do the things he commands and refrain from the things he forbids.

Story: The Scholar Who Said "Allah Does Not Exist" and the Response of Imam Abu Hanifa:

Once upon a time in Baghdad, there lived a great man. His name was Imam al-A'zam (the Greatest Imam) Abu Hanifa. He was a world-famous scholar. He taught many students. Everybody in his area showed him respect.

Even in those days, there was an unthinking man who considered himself a scholar and claimed "There is no God." Everywhere he went he argued with the scholars.

The scholar mentioned here had also heard of the fame of Abu Hanifa. He wanted to put his argument and claim before him. Intending to do this, he went to Baghdad. He found Abu Hanifa and made his claim by asking, "Does Allah exist? or not?" Abu Hanifa did not immediately respond to this claim. He said that they would meet the next day at a particular time at the same place and he himself would answer.

As you know, the Tigris River passes through the middle of Baghdad and cuts the city in two.

The next day Abu Hanifa did not come at the specified time to the meeting place. The man who considered himself a scholar became bored. When he was just about ready to leave, Abu Hanifa came to the meeting place. The claimant said to Abu Hanifa:

- Why did you come late? Were you that afraid to argue with me?

Abu Hanifa said, laughing at his words:

- No. I wasn't afraid. You surely know I live on the other side of the river. There is also no bridge nearby to use to cross over from that side to here. I was hoping that really quickly some bridge would get itself built without a craftsman or an architect. Thus, it spontaneously happened, but its happening took a little time. I passed over that bridge, so I became late. Now I've come.

The liar said:

- You're lying. Has there ever been a bridge that came about with no craftsman and no architect? Is believing that not lunacy?

Abu Hanifa replied:

- O man! Seeing that there can't be a bridge that comes about spontaneously, how can this world exist by itself without any craftsman? In this world, without rhyme or reason, not even a leaf has spontaneously moved. You still can't make head or tail of there being a reason for everything?

Faced with these words, the man who considered himself a scholar understood his mistake. He realized that the maker of this world exists. Apologizing, he gave up his claim. He believed in Allah's existence and his oneness.

Belief in Angels *(Mala'ik)*

Characteristics of angels:

a) Angels are absolutely pure, noble beings, created from light. They are neither masculine, nor feminine, and they do not marry, eat, or drink.

b) Angels are not seen.

c) Angels do not know the unseen. If Allah teaches them something, they know it.

The Duties of Angels:

The duties of angels are to praise Allah, sing his praise (describing the greatness of His glory), and do whatever they are commanded.

The Duties of the Four Great Angels:

1- Jabra'il (Gabriel): He is the bearer of revelation and the holy books to the prophets.

2- Mika'il (Michael): He looks after natural events (like rain and wind).

3- Israfil: He is given the duty of blowing the trumpet at the Resurrection.

4- Azra'il (Azrael): The duty of taking life belongs to this angel.

These are the greatest of the angels. Allah's commands to the other angels are reached through these angels.

Some Other Angels and Their Duties:

Kiraman Kitabin: To the right and left of every person, there is an angel that records everything they say and do. The one on the right records good deeds in writing, the one on the left bad deeds. These books will be given to the owner on the Day of Judgment.

The reckoning will be done according to these books.

Munkar and Nakir: These angels are given the duty of questioning those placed in the grave.

Story: **How Can Azrail Kill Thousands of People at the Same Time?**

Dear children! You've also been curious about this. We can liken our spirit to a burning light bulb, and death to the bulb's burning out. The electric lines that come to our house are connected to an electric power plant, are they not?

Do you know what would happen if some engineer at the power plant were to tell someone working there, “Turn off the power at such-and-such neighborhood”? He would cut off power to the specified sector and, in an instant, tens of thousands of lights would be shut off.

Looking at this, we can think of Azrail of having switches in front of him connected to the invisible power cords of our souls. In this case, it is a matter of an instant that, by moving one finger, Azrail makes thousands of souls fade out and go away.

Belief in the Scriptures *(Kutub)*

The divine and heavenly scriptures were sent by Allah to the prophets by way of revelation (*wahy*).

Wahy: *Wahy* (revelation) is Allah’s communication with His servants selected from among the people as prophets, through the Angel Jabrail.

Wahy is only received by the prophets.

Some of the scriptures sent by Allah are called “*suhuf* (pages/scrolls)” because they are small scriptures of only a few pages. For example:

Adam’s 10 pages.
Shith’s (Seth) 50 pages.
Idris’s 30 pages.
Ibrahim’s 10 pages.
None of these pages are existent today.

The Great Books are Four:

1- ***The Torah (at-Tawrat)*** - This was revealed to Moses.
2- ***The Psalms (az-Zabur)***- These were revealed to David.
3- ***The Gospel*** **(*Injil*)**- This was revealed to Jesus.

4- *The "Noble" Quran*: This was revealed by God, through the Angel Gabriel, to the Prophet Muhammad. (Peace be upon all the prophets). The only book that is protected and preserved as it came from Allah is *The Quran*.

The Quran was revealed not only for reading it to the dead, like some ignorant Muslims view it today. It was not revealed so it could be read to the sick, and at graves and shrines, without its meaning and principles being understood. *The Quran* includes principles that encompass all of a Muslim's life, from the cradle to the grave. A Muslim should arrange all his personal, family, and worldly life according to the principles of *The Quran*, and it is necessary that he or she conform to them.

The Quran was finished in 23 years and it is 114 *surahs*.

Belief in the Prophets

Prophets are the people chosen and appointed by Allah to make known to his servants everything that He wishes.

Characteristics That Must Be Found in Prophets:

1- ***Sidq*:** This means veracity or truthfulness. Prophets are truthful to the highest degree, honest people.

2- ***Amanah*:** Prophets are, in all respects, men to be relied upon and trusted.

3- ***Tabligh*:** Prophets must bring the religion and law sent by Allah as it is to the people.

4- ***Fatanah*:** Prophets must be people of high intellect and intelligence.

5- ***'Ismah*:** Prophets are far from sin and evil.

The Number of the Prophets:

The first prophet was Adam (pbuh) and the last was Muhammad (pbuh). Between these two, many prophets came and went. All prophets called the people to servitude of Allah and belief in His oneness (*tawhid*). When people went astray and worshipped other than Allah, they had a new prophet sent to them, calling them to belief in Allah's oneness.

Prophets Mentioned by Name in *The Quran*:

The Prophets mentioned in *The Quran* are twenty-five:

Adam	Ibrahim (Abraham)	Musa (Moses)	Yunus (Jonah)
Idris	Ismail (Ishmael)	Harun (Aaron)	Ilyas (Elijah)
Nuh (Noah)	Ishaq (Isaac)	Davud (David)	Alyasa (Elisha)
Hud	Yakub (Jacob)	Sulayman (Solomon)	Zakariyya (Zechariah)
Salih	Yusuf (Joseph)	Ayyub (Job)	Yahya (John)
Lut (Lot)	Shu'ayb	Dhu l-Kifl	'Isa (Jesus)
Muhammad (pbuh)			

***Mu'jizah* (Miracle):** *Mu'jizah* means to leave one weak and powerless. Miracles are supernatural feats carried out by prophets, with Allah's consent and help, to prove their prophethood. Regular people, under the same circumstances, do not have the power to bring about similar things.

Belief in the Hereafter *(al-Akhirah)*

***Yawm al-akhira* (The Last Day):** According to one account, when the *sur* (trumpet) is blown by Israfil, all living things will fall and die. The time starting then and continuing through the resurrection of people, the entering into paradise of those bound for paradise, and the entering of hell for those bound for hell, is called "The Last Day."

According to another account, the hereafter (*al-akhira*) starts when people begin to be resurrected so they can be called to account for their deeds, and continues forever. There are other names for *al-akhira*, but "*yawm al-qiyamah* (The Day of Resurrection)," is the most famous.

***Hayat al-Qabr* (Life in the Grave):** The life in the grave begins with the death of a person and continues until his resurrection. After being placed in the grave, two angels come and ask, "Who is your Lord? Who is your prophet? And what is your religion?" These are called the questions of the grave. These questions will be asked of everybody. People with bodies that have disintegrated or burned to ashes will also be asked.

The life in the grave means the start of the hereafter. People bound for heaven and people bound for hell will begin to taste the sweetness of the life in heaven or the punishment of hell respectively to a lesser or greater degree.

The life in the grave should not be compared with the life of this world.

However, in sleep (which is called the "little death") we can taste with our souls joyous pleasure or miserable pain, thus seeing an example of *al-akhirah* in this life.

***Jannah* (Paradise)** is a place of reward. It has been made for the *mu'mins* (believers). In an *ayah*, it says "therein you shall have all that your souls desire, all that you call for" (Quran, 41:31, Arberry translation).

***Jahannam* (Hell)** is the place of punishment for those who rebel and go against Allah. Those who die whose sins are great and those believers deemed unworthy of intercession, go there along with unbelievers and hypocrites. While believers who enter will be taken out after a punishment of a specified time, unbelievers, hypocrites, and polytheists will remain permanently.

***Mahshar*:** With the blowing of Israfil's trumpet, all people and creatures will fall and die. Except for Allah, no living existence will continue. For a time it will stay like this. Then Allah will resurrect Israfil. Israfil will then blow his trumpet again and people will then be given life again in an instant. They will gather in *Mahshar* for their reckoning.

The Book of Deeds: In *Mahshar*, people will be given their books (the books the angels wrote and prepared in this world). The people bound for heaven will be given their books from the right, while the people bound for hell will be given their books from the left.

***Hasab* (Reckoning):** Allah will take all people to account at the same time. But each person will think that only his own reckoning is being done. This reckoning will be as our Prophet (pbuh) explained:

Everyone will be asked:

1- How they spent their lives
2- What they did with what they know
3- Where they got their wealth from and where they spent it (*halal* or *haram*).
4- And which roads (roads that are either pleasing or unpleasing to Allah) they wore out their bodies on,

And an answer will surely be given.

***al-Mizan* (The Balance):** This is the weighing of peoples' good and bad deeds.

Nobody will be wronged in any way. Every good or bad thing done will surely be placed on the balance. Each good deed will count for ten and every bad deed will count as one.

as-Sirat **(The Narrow Bridge):** This is a way, a bridge, that everyone must take: those who will be placed in hell, those believers who will reach heaven, polytheists, unbelievers, and hypocrites who will fall to hell. The ease or difficulty of the passing will be according to the rank of servitude to Allah in this world.

We came here for worship; we will return for reckoning.

We are guests on this earth; we will die to be brought back to life.

Story: **The Story of the Bringing to Life of Four Birds**

Ibrahim (pbuh) was telling everybody, "My Lord causes death and life," and he sincerely believed this himself. Despite that, one day Ibrahim supplicated to Allah, saying:

- O my Lord! Show me how you will bring the dead to life!

Allah Almighty said to him:

- Did you stop believing that I'm going to resurrect the dead, or what?

Ibrahim said:

- I certainly believe, my Lord! But let me see with my eyes so my heart may rest soundly.

In reply to this, Allah said to Ibrahim:

- So, get four birds! Acquaint yourself with them well! When you call them by name they will fly to you. Then, slaughter them!

Chop the meat up and mix them together well! Separate this meat into four parts and put each part on the top of a mountain! Then call them in the way they are used to! You'll see them hurry to you. After you see this, then believe well that Allah's power is enough to do everything and he does nothing in vain, he does it knowingly.

Ibrahim was very happy that his wish was granted. Right

away he took a pigeon, a peacock, a crow and a rooster and got them used to him. Wherever these animals were, immediately upon hearing Ibrahim's voice, they flew straight to him.

One day, in the way he was commanded, he slaughtered them. After mixing the meat together well, he separated it into four parts. He put each part on the top of a mountain. Then he retired to an appropriate place. Then he called the birds and rooster in the same way they were used to. In an instant, the resurrected, living animals flew straight to him.

Seeing this, Ibrahim fell directly into prostration and thanked his Lord. His belief in Him was strengthened even more.

Belief in *Qadar* and *Qada*

Description of *Qadar*: Allah's knowing, from pre-eternity to post-eternity (with no beginning and no end), the time and place of things, and when they will be, all of them, and His decreeing in pre-eternity (while they have not yet come into existence) their determination and predestination, is called *Qadar*, and this is related to Allah's attribute of knowledge.

Everything is obligated to be as it was predestined by Allah in pre-eternity. The coming about of nothing was left to petty chance.

Description of *Qada*: *Qaza* is the coming about of everything (when the time comes for the determined, predestined thing to be) according to the way it was decreed in pre-eternity. The one who predestines things is Allah. The one who brings about everything according to the way it was predestined is also Allah. Therefore, there is complete agreement between *qadar* and *qada*. If *qadar* is a plan, it may be said that *qada* is the work of bringing it about.

The Deeds of People and Their Accountability for Them:

a) Acts Done Outside the Will of People:

Our will has no effect on matters like our birth, the time of our death, and our gender. We are not answerable for these things.

b) Acts Related to the Wills of People:

The things that Allah destines that are related to our wills, are carried out as things connected to our wills. While Allah holds us responsible for this, it is not to force us to do something, then ask "Why did you do it?" Therefore, He left us free to our own wills and desires so we could be held accountable. This is like a chauffeur who, with the power that comes from the motor, can turn the bus to the right, to the left, or lead it straight ahead. When he wants, he can step on the brakes and stop the bus. If he causes an accident, he isn't asked, "Why was power coming from the engine?" Rather, he is asked "Why were you speeding? Why were you turning to the left and right? And why didn't you stop?"

Khayr and *Sharr* (Good and Bad)

Khayr **(Good):** *Khayr* is something that is beneficial to someone, with respect to its result.

Sharr **(Bad/Evil):** *Sharr* is something that is harmful to someone. Since there is no other creator besides Allah, the creator of good and the creator of bad are both Him. It says in *The Quran* "Allah is the creator of everything." In our religion, good things are commanded, and bad things are forbidden.

The Wisdom of the Creation of *Sharr*:

a) In the creation even of the bad and evil things that we see, there is a wisdom from Allah that we do not know. Something that seems harmful or bad for some people may be beneficial for others or with respect to the public.

b) Bad helps us to understand the value of good. Someone

who has never been sick does not understand the value of health.

Our Situation with Respect to *Khayr* (Good) and *Sharr* (Evil) :

We should be thankful when faced with good; when faced with evil, we should be patient and try to recover from it.

The Matter of (*Rizq*) Sustenance (Our Daily Bread): Allah is also the one who provides every living thing with the sustenance that it needs to live. Yet the searching for and finding of food is the duty of people. A person has an effect on whether the sustenance that comes to him is from *halal* or *haram* sources.

The Matter of the Time of Death (*Ajal*): *Ajal* is the designated time for the span of a person's life. After a person's time comes, whether they be young or old, healthy or sick, or whatever the situation, he or she will die as destined by Allah. The *ayah* which says, "when their term comes they shall not put it back by a single hour nor put it forward (Quran 10:49, Arberry)," states that the *ajal* will not change.

Readings of *Surahs* for the *Salah* (Prayer)

Note: You should not memorize the readings of the *surahs* for the prayer by reading their Latin transliterations because the transliterations do not completely express the Arabic.

Subhanaka

سُبْحَانَكَ اَللّٰهُمَّ وَبِحَمْدِكَ وَتَبَارَكَ اسْمُكَ وَتَعَالٰى جَدُّكَ (وَجَلَّ ثَنَآؤُكَ) وَ لَآ اِلٰهَ غَيْرُكَ .

Subhanaka Allahumma wa bi hamdik. Wa tabaraka smuk. Wa t'ala jadduk. (Wa jalla thana'uk). Wa la ilaha ghayruk.*

* This part is only read in the funeral (*janazah*) prayer.

Translation: Glory be to You, O Allah! Praise be to You. Blessed be Your name, and exalted be Your majesty. (Innumerable is Your praise). There is no god besides You.

At-Tahiyyat

اَلتَّحِيَّاتُ لِلّٰهِ وَالصَّلَوَاتُ وَالطَّيِّبَاتُ اَلسَّلَامُ عَلَيْكَ اَيُّهَا النَّبِىُّ وَرَحْمَةُ اللّٰهِ وَبَرَكَاتُهُ اَلسَّلَامُ عَلَيْنَاوَعَلٰى عِبَادِاللّٰهِ الصَّالِحِينَ اَشْهَدُ اَنْ لَآ اِلٰهَ اِلَّا اللّٰهُ وَاَشْهَدُ اَنَّ مُحَمَّدًاعَبْدُهُ وَرَسُولُهُ .

At-tahiyyatu lillahi wa s-salawatu wa t-tayyibat. As-salamu 'alayka ayyuha n-nabiyyu wa rahmatullahi wa barakatuh. As-salamu 'alayna wa 'ala 'ibadillahi s-salihin. Ashhadu an la ilaha illa Allah. Wa ashhadu anna Muhammadan 'abduhu wa rasuluh.

Translation: All salutations, prayers, and goodness belong to Allah. Peace be upon you, O Prophet, and the mercy of Allah and His blessings. Peace be upon us, and upon the upright servants of Allah. I bear witness that there is no god, but Allah. And I bear witness that Muhammad is his servant and Messenger.

Allahumma Salli

اَللّٰهُمَّ صَلِّ عَلٰى مُحَمَّدٍ وَ عَلٰى اٰلِ مُحَمَّدٍ كَمَا صَلَّيْتَ

عَلٰى اِبْرَاهِيمَ وَ عَلٰى اٰلِ اِبْرَاهِيمَ اِنَّكَ حَمِيدٌ مَجِيدٌ.

Allahumma salli 'ala sayyidina Muhammadin wa 'ala ali sayyidina Muhammad, kama sallayta 'ala Ibrahima wa 'ala ali Ibrahim. Innaka hamidun majid.

Translation: O Allah! Have mercy upon Muhammad and upon the family of Muhammad as you had mercy on Ibrahim and on the family of Ibrahim. Verily, you are glorious and worthy of praise.

Allahumma Barik

اَللّٰهُمَّ بَارِكْ عَلٰى مُحَمَّدٍ وَ عَلٰى اٰلِ مُحَمَّدٍ كَمَا بَارَكْتَ

عَلٰى اِبْرَاهِيمَ وَ عَلٰى اٰلِ اِبْرَاهِيمَ اِنَّكَ حَمِيدٌ مَجِيدٌ.

Allahumma barik 'ala sayyidina Muhammadin wa 'ala ali Muhammad, kama barakta 'ala Ibrahima wa 'ala ali Ibrahim. Innaka hamidun majid.

Translation: O Allah! Bless Muhammad and the family of Muhammad, as you blessed Ibrahim and the family of Ibrahim. Verily, you are glorious and worthy of praise.

Rabbana

رَبَّنَآ اٰتِنَا فِي الدُّنْيَا حَسَنَةً وَ فِي الْاٰخِرَةِ حَسَنَةً وَقِنَا عَذَابَ النَّارِ ۞
رَبَّنَا اغْفِرْ لِي وَ لِوَالِدَيَّ وَ لِلْمُؤْمِنِينَ يَوْمَ يَقُومُ الْحِسَابِ ۞

Rabbana atina fi d-dunya hasanatan wa fi l-akhirati hasanatan wa qina 'adhaba n-nar. Rabbana ghfirli wa li walidayya wa lil-mu'minina yawma yaqumu l-hisab.

Translation: O my Lord, grant us goodness in this life, and goodness in the hereafter, and save us from the punishment of the Fire. O my Lord, forgive me, my parents, and the believers, on the day of the reckoning.

Qunut Duas

اَللّٰهُمَّ إِنَّا نَسْتَعِينُكَ وَ نَسْتَغْفِرُكَ وَ نَسْتَهْدِيكَ وَ نُؤْمِنُ بِكَ وَ نَتُوبُ
اِلَيْكَ وَ نَتَوَكَّلُ عَلَيْكَ وَ نُثْنِي عَلَيْكَ الْخَيْرَ كُلَّهُ نَشْكُرُكَ
وَ لَا نَكْفُرُكَ وَ نَخْلَعُ وَ نَتْرُكُ مَنْ يَفْجُرُكَ.

Allahumma inna nasta'inuka va nastaghfiruka wa nastahdik. Wa nu'minu bika wa natubu ilayk. Wa natawakkalu 'alayka wa nuthni 'alayka l-khayra kullahu nashkuruka wa la nakfuruk. Wa nakhla'u wa natruku man yafjuruk.

Translation: O Allah, we ask You for help, forgiveness, and guidance. We believe in You and turn towards You. We trust in You and we praise You with all goodness. We thank You and we do not show ingratitude. We leave and abandon any who go against you.

اَللّٰهُمَّ اِيَّاكَ نَعْبُدُ وَ لَكَ نُصَلِّى وَ نَسْجُدُ وَ اِلَيْكَ نَسعٰى وَ نَحفِدُ نَرْجُو رَحْمَتَكَ وَ نَخْشٰى عَذَابَكَ اِنَّ عَذَابَكَ بِالْكُفَّارِ مُلْحِقٌ.

Allahumma iyyaka na'budu wa laka nusalli wa nasjudu wa ilayka nas'a wa nahfidu narju rahmataka wa nakhsha 'adhabak. Inna 'adhabaka bi l-kuffari mulhiq.

Translation: O Allah, we worship You, we pray to You, we prostrate to You, and we strive for You in haste. We hope for Your mercy and we fear Your punishment. Verily, Your punishment will be inflicted upon the unbelievers.

Ayat al-Kursi

بِسْمِ اللّٰهِ الرَّحْمَنِ الرَّحِيمِ ۞ اللَّهُ لاَ إِلَـهَ إِلاَّ هُوَ الْحَيُّ الْقَيُّومُ لاَ تَأْخُذُهُ سِنَةٌ وَلاَ نَوْمٌ لَّهُ مَا فِي السَّمَاوَاتِ وَمَا فِي الأَرْضِ مَن ذَا الَّذِي يَشْفَعُ عِنْدَهُ إِلاَّ بِإِذْنِهِ يَعْلَمُ مَا بَيْنَ أَيْدِيهِمْ وَمَا خَلْفَهُمْ وَلاَ يُحِيطُونَ بِشَيْءٍ مِّنْ عِلْمِهِ إِلاَّ بِمَا شَاء وَسِعَ كُرْسِيُّهُ السَّمَاوَاتِ وَالأَرْضَ وَلاَ يَؤُودُهُ حِفْظُهُمَا وَهُوَ الْعَلِيُّ الْعَظِيمُ

Allahu la ilaha illa huwa l-hayyu l-qayyum. La ta'khudhuhu sinatuwwa la nawm. Lahu ma fi s-samawati wa ma fi l-ard. Man dhalladhi yashfa'u 'indahu illa bi idhnihi. Ya'lamu ma bayna aydihim wa ma khalfahum. Wa la yuhituna bi shayimmin 'ilmihi illa bima sha'. Wasi'a kursiyyuhu s-samawati wa l-ard. Wa la ya'uduhu hifzuhuma wa huwa l-'aliyyu l-'azim.

Translation: Allah! There is no deity save Him, the Alive, the Eternal. Neither slumber nor sleep overtaketh Him. Unto Him belongeth whatsoever is in the heavens and whatsoever is in the earth. Who is he that intercedeth with Him save by His leave? He knoweth that which is in front of them and that which is behind them, while they encompass nothing of His knowledge save what He will. His throne includeth the heavens and the earth, and He is never weary of preserving them. He is the Sublime, the Tremendous. (Quran 2:255, Pickthall).

Surat al-Fatihah

Bismillahi r-Rahmani r-Rahim. Al-Hamdu lillahi rabbi l-'alamin. Ar-Rahmani r-Rahim. Maliki yawmi d-din. Iyyaka na'budu wa iyyaka nasta'in. Ihdina s-sirata l-mustaqim. Sirata lladhina an'amta 'alayhim, ghayri l-maghdubi 'alayhim wa la d-dallin.

بِسْمِ اللّٰهِ الرَّحْمٰنِ الرَّحِيمِ

اَلْحَمْدُ لِلّٰهِ رَبِّ الْعَالَمِينَ ﴿٢﴾ الرَّحْمٰنِ الرَّحِيمِ ﴿٣﴾ مَالِكِ يَوْمِ الدِّينِ ﴿٤﴾ إِيَّاكَ نَعْبُدُ وإِيَّاكَ نَسْتَعِينُ ﴿٥﴾ اِهْدِنَــا الصِّرَاطَ الْمُسْتَقِيمَ ﴿٦﴾ صِرَاطَ الَّذِينَ أَنْعَمْتَ عَلَيْهِمْ غَيْرِ الْمَغْضُوبِ عَلَيْهِمْ وَلَا الضَّالِّينَ ﴿٧﴾

Translation: In the name of Allah, the Beneficent, the Merciful. Praise be to Allah, Lord of the Worlds, The Beneficent, the Merciful. Master of the Day of Judgment, Thee (alone) we worship; Thee (alone) we ask for help. Show us the straight path, The path of those whom Thou hast favoured; Not the (path) of those who earn Thine anger nor of those who go astray. (Quran 1, Pickthall).

Surat an-Nas

Qul a'udhu bi rabbi n-nas, Maliki n-nas, Ilahi n-nas, min sharri l-waswasi l-khannas, alladhi yuwaswisu fi suduri n-nas, min al-jinnati wa n-nas.

Translation: Say: I seek refuge in the Lord of mankind, The King of mankind, The god of mankind, From the evil of the sneaking whisperer, Who whispereth in the hearts of mankind, Of the jinn and of mankind. (Quran 114, Pickthall).

بِسْمِ اللّٰهِ الرَّحْمَنِ الرَّحِيمِ

قُلْ أَعُوذُ بِرَبِّ النَّاسِ ﴿١﴾
مَلِكِ النَّاسِ ﴿٢﴾ إِلَهِ النَّاسِ ﴿٣﴾
مِن شَرِّ الْوَسْوَاسِ الْخَنَّاسِ ﴿٤﴾
الَّذِي يُوَسْوِسُ فِي صُدُورِ
النَّاسِ ﴿٥﴾ مِنَ الْجِنَّةِ وَ النَّاسِ ﴿٦﴾

Surat al-Falaq

Qul a'udhu bi Rabbi l-falaq, min sharri ma khalaq, wa min sharri ghasiqin idha waqab, wa min sharri n-naffathati fi l-'uqad, wa min sharri hasidin idha hasad.

Translation: Say: I seek refuge in the Lord of the Daybreak, From the evil of that which He created; From the evil of the darkness when it is intense, And from the evil of malignant witchcraft, And from the evil of the envier when he envieth. (Quran 113, Pickthall).

بِسْمِ اللّٰهِ الرَّحْمَنِ الرَّحِيمِ

قُلْ أَعُوذُ بِرَبِّ الْفَلَقِ ﴿١﴾ مِن شَرِّ
مَا خَلَقَ ﴿٢﴾ وَمِن شَرِّ غَاسِقٍ إِذَا
وَقَبَ ﴿٣﴾ وَمِن شَرِّ النَّفَّاثَاتِ فِي
الْعُقَدِ ﴿٤﴾ وَمِن شَرِّ حَاسِدٍ إِذَا
حَسَدَ ﴿٥﴾

Surat al-Ikhlas

بِسْمِ اللَّهِ الرَّحْمَنِ الرَّحِيمِ

قُلْ هُوَ اللَّهُ أَحَدٌ ﴿١﴾ اللَّهُ الصَّمَدُ ﴿٢﴾ لَمْ يَلِدْ وَلَمْ يُولَدْ ﴿٣﴾ وَلَمْ يَكُن لَّهُ كُفُواً أَحَدٌ ﴿٤﴾

Qul huwa Allahu ahad, Allahu samad. Lam yalid wa lam yulad. Wa lam yakullahu kufuwan ahad.

Translation: Say: He is Allah, the One! Allah, the eternally Besought of all! He begetteth not nor was begotten. And there is none comparable unto Him. (Quran 112, Pickthall).

Surat at-Masad

بِسْمِ اللَّهِ الرَّحْمَنِ الرَّحِيمِ

تَبَّتْ يَدَا أَبِي لَهَبٍ وَتَبَّ ﴿١﴾ مَا أَغْنَى عَنْهُ مَالُهُ وَمَا كَسَبَ ﴿٢﴾ سَيَصْلَى نَاراً ذَاتَ لَهَبٍ ﴿٣﴾ وَامْرَأَتُهُ حَمَّالَةَ الْحَطَبِ ﴿٤﴾ فِي جِيدِهَا حَبْلٌ مِّن مَّسَدٍ ﴿٥﴾

Tabbat yada Abi Lahabiwwatab. Ma aghna 'anhu ma lahu wama kasab. Sayasla naran dhata lahab. Wamra'tuhu hammalata l-hatab. Fi jidiha hablummin masad.

Translation: The power of Abu Lahab will perish, and he will perish. His wealth and gains will not exempt him. He will be plunged in flaming Fire, And his wife, the wood-carrier, Will have upon her neck a halter of palm-fibre. (Quran 111, Pickthall).

Surat an-Nasr

Idha ja'a nasrullahi wa l-fath. Wa ra'ayta n-nasa yadkhuluna fi dinillahi afwaja. Fasabbih bi hamdi Rabbika wastaghfirhu, innahu kana tawwaba.

Translation: When Allah's succor and the triumph cometh And thou seest mankind entering the religion of Allah in troops, Then hymn the raises of thy Lord, and seek forgiveness of Him. Lo! He is ever ready to show mercy. (Quran 110, Pickthall).

بِسْمِ اللّٰهِ الرَّحْمَنِ الرَّحِيم

إِذَا جَاءَ نَصْرُ اللَّهِ وَالْفَتْحُ ﴿١﴾
وَرَأَيْتَ النَّاسَ يَدْخُلُونَ فِي دِينِ
اللَّهِ أَفْوَاجاً ﴿٢﴾ فَسَبِّحْ بِحَمْدِ
رَبِّكَ وَاسْتَغْفِرْهُ إِنَّهُ كَانَ تَوَّاباً ﴿٣﴾

Surat al-Kafirun

Qul ya ayyuha l-kafirun. La a'budu ma ta'budun. Wa la antum 'abiduna ma a'bud. Wa la ana 'abidumma 'abadtum. Wala antum 'abiduna ma a'bud. Lakum dinukum wa liya din.

Translation: Say: O disbelievers! I worship not that which ye worship; Nor worship ye that which I worship. And I shall not worship that which ye worship. Nor will ye worship that which I worship. Unto you your religion, and unto me my religion. (Quran 109, Pickthall).

بِسْمِ اللّٰهِ الرَّحْمَنِ الرَّحِيم

قُلْ يَا أَيُّهَا الْكَافِرُونَ ﴿١﴾ لَا
أَعْبُدُ مَا تَعْبُدُونَ ﴿٢﴾ وَلَا أَنتُمْ
عَابِدُونَ مَا أَعْبُدُ ﴿٣﴾ وَلَا أَنَا
عَابِدٌ مَّا عَبَدتُّمْ ﴿٤﴾ وَلَا أَنتُمْ
عَابِدُونَ مَا أَعْبُدُ ﴿٥﴾ لَكُمْ
دِينُكُمْ وَلِيَ دِينِ ﴿٦﴾

Surat al-Kawthar

بِسْمِ اللَّهِ الرَّحْمَنِ الرَّحِيمِ

إِنَّا أَعْطَيْنَاكَ الْكَوْثَرَ ﴿١﴾ فَصَلِّ لِرَبِّكَ وَانْحَرْ ﴿٢﴾ إِنَّ شَانِئَكَ هُوَ الْأَبْتَرُ ﴿٣﴾

Inna a'taynaka l-Kawthar. Fasalli li Rabbika wanhar. Inna shani'aka huwa l-abtar.

Translation: Lo! We have given thee Abundance; So pray unto thy Lord, and sacrifice. Lo! It is thy insulter (and not thou) who is without posterity. (Quran 108, Pickthall).

Surat al-Ma'un

بِسْمِ اللَّهِ الرَّحْمَنِ الرَّحِيمِ

أَرَأَيْتَ الَّذِي يُكَذِّبُ بِالدِّينِ ﴿١﴾ فَذَلِكَ الَّذِي يَدُعُّ الْيَتِيمَ ﴿٢﴾ وَلَا يَحُضُّ عَلَى طَعَامِ الْمِسْكِينِ ﴿٣﴾ فَوَيْلٌ لِّلْمُصَلِّينَ ﴿٤﴾ الَّذِينَ هُمْ عَن صَلَاتِهِمْ سَاهُونَ ﴿٥﴾ الَّذِينَ هُمْ يُرَاؤُونَ ﴿٦﴾ وَيَمْنَعُونَ الْمَاعُونَ ﴿٧﴾

Ara'ayta lladhi yukadhdhibu bi d-din. Fadhalika lladhi yadu'u l-yatim. Wa la yahuddu 'ala ta'ami l-miskin. Fa waylulli l-musallin. Alladhinahum 'an salatihim sahun. Alladhinahum yura'un, wa yamna'una l-ma'un.

Translation: Hast thou observed him who belieth religion? That is he who repelleth the orphan, And urgeth not the feeding of the needy. Ah, woe unto worshippers Who are heedless of their prayer; Who would be seen (at worship) Yet refuse small kindnesses! (Quran 107, Pickthall).

Surat al-Quraysh

بِسْمِ اللهِ الرَّحْمَنِ الرَّحِيمِ

لِإِيلَافِ قُرَيْشٍ ﴿١﴾ إِيلَافِهِمْ رِحْلَةَ
الشِّتَاءِ وَالصَّيْفِ ﴿٢﴾ فَلْيَعْبُدُوا
رَبَّ هَٰذَا الْبَيْتِ ﴿٣﴾ الَّذِي
أَطْعَمَهُم مِّن جُوعٍ وَآمَنَهُم
مِّنْ خَوْفٍ ﴿٤﴾

Li ilafi Qurayshin, ilafihim rihlata sh-shita'i wa s-sayf. Falya'budu rabba hadha l-bayti lladhi at'amahum min ju'iwwa amanahum min khawf.

Translation: For the taming of Qureysh. For their taming (We cause) the caravans to set forth in winter and summer. So let them worship the Lord of this House, Who hath fed them against hunger and hath made them safe from fear. (Quran 106, Pickthall).

Surat al-Fil

بِسْمِ اللهِ الرَّحْمَنِ الرَّحِيمِ

أَلَمْ تَرَ كَيْفَ فَعَلَ رَبُّكَ
بِأَصْحَابِ الْفِيلِ ﴿١﴾ أَلَمْ يَجْعَلْ
كَيْدَهُمْ فِي تَضْلِيلٍ ﴿٢﴾
وَأَرْسَلَ عَلَيْهِمْ طَيْرًا أَبَابِيلَ ﴿٣﴾
تَرْمِيهِم بِحِجَارَةٍ مِّن سِجِّيلٍ ﴿٤﴾
فَجَعَلَهُمْ كَعَصْفٍ مَّأْكُولٍ ﴿٥﴾

Alam tara kayfa fa'ala rabbuka bi ashabi l-fil. Alam yaj'al kaydahum fi tadlil. Wa arsala 'alayhim tayran ababil. Tarmihim bihijaratim min sijjil. Faja'alahum ka'asfim ma'kul.

Translation: Hast thou not seen how thy Lord dealt with the owners of the Elephant? Did He not bring their stratagem to naught, And send against them swarms of flying creatures, Which pelted them with stones of baked clay, And made them like green crops devoured (by cattle)? (Quran 105, Pickthall).

www.ingramcontent.com/pod-product-compliance
Lightning Source LLC
Chambersburg PA
CBHW062144160726
48282CB00027B/942
9789366080307